# BASEBALL LEGENDS

Hank Aaron
Grover Cleveland Alexander
Ernie Banks
Johnny Bench
Yogi Berra
Roy Campanella
Roberto Clemente
Ty Cobb
Dizzy Dean
Joe DiMaggio
Bob Feller
Jimmie Foxx
Lou Gehrig
Bob Gibson
Rogers Hornsby
Walter Johnson
Sandy Koufax
Mickey Mantle
Christy Mathewson
Willie Mays
Stan Musial
Satchel Paige
Brooks Robinson
Frank Robinson
Jackie Robinson
Babe Ruth
Tom Seaver
Duke Snider
Warren Spahn
Willie Stargell
Honus Wagner
Ted Williams
Carl Yastrzemski
Cy Young

CHELSEA HOUSE PUBLISHERS

BASEBALL LEGENDS

# TY COBB

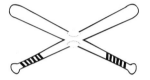

*Norman L. Macht*

*Introduction by*
*Jim Murray*

*Senior Consultant*
*Earl Weaver*

## CHELSEA HOUSE PUBLISHERS
*New York • Philadelphia*

**CHELSEA HOUSE PUBLISHERS**

*Editor-in-Chief:* Richard S. Papale
*Managing Editor:* Karyn Gullen Browne
*Copy Chief:* Philip Koslow
*Picture Editor:* Adrian G. Allen
*Art Director:* Nora Wertz
*Manufacturing Director:* Gerald Levine
*Systems Manager:* Lindsey Ottman
*Production Coordinator:* Marie Claire Cebrián-Ume

**Baseball Legends**
*Senior Editor:* Richard Rennert

**Staff for TY COBB**
*Copy Editor:* David Carter
*Designer:* Diana Blume
*Picture Researcher:* Alan Gottlieb
*Cover Illustration:* Daniel O'Leary
*Editorial Assistant:* Laura Petermann

3  5  7  9  8  6  4

Library of Congress Cataloging-in-Publication Data
Macht, Norman L.
Ty Cobb/Norman L. Macht.
p.  cm.—(Baseball legends)
Includes bibliographical references and index.
ISBN 0-7910-1172-0
0-7910-1206-9 (pbk)
1. Cobb, Ty, 1886–1961.   2. Baseball players—United
States—Biography.     I. Title.   II. Series.
GV865.C6M27     1992
796.357'092—dc20
[B]

91-39786
CIP

# CONTENTS

WHAT MAKES A STAR  6
Jim Murray

CHAPTER 1
PLAYING TO WIN  9

CHAPTER 2
THE BASEBALL BUG  15

CHAPTER 3
"DON'T COME HOME A FAILURE"  21

CHAPTER 4
THE HOT-TEMPERED ROOKIE  29

CHAPTER 5
FLASHING SPIKES  35

CHAPTER 6
WEALTHY, FAMOUS, AND LONELY  41

CHAPTER 7
A FIGHTER TO THE END  49

CHRONOLOGY  59
STATISTICS  61
FURTHER READING  62
INDEX  63

# WHAT MAKES A STAR

*Jim Murray*

No one has ever been able to explain to me the mysterious alchemy that makes one man a .350 hitter and another player, more or less identical in physical makeup, hard put to hit .200. You look at an Al Kaline, who played with the Detroit Tigers from 1953 to 1974. He was pale, stringy, almost poetic-looking. He always seemed to be struggling against a bad case of mononucleosis. But with a bat in his hands, he was King Kong. During his career, he hit 399 home runs, rapped out 3,007 hits, and compiled a .297 batting average.

Form isn't the reason. The first time anybody saw Roberto Clemente step into the batter's box for the Pittsburgh Pirates, the best guess was that Clemente would be back in Double A ball in a week. He had one foot in the bucket and held his bat at an awkward angle—he looked as though he couldn't hit an outside pitch. A lot of other ballplayers may have had a better-looking stance. Yet they never led the National League in hitting in four different years, the way Clemente did.

Not every ballplayer is born with the ability to hit a curveball. Nor is exceptional hand-eye coordination the key to heavy hitting. Big-league locker rooms are filled with players who have all the attributes, save one: discipline. Every baseball man can tell you a story about a pitcher who throws a ball faster than anyone has ever seen but who has no control on or *off* the field.

The Hall of Fame is full of people who transformed themselves into great ballplayers by working at the sport, by studying the game, and making sacrifices. They're overachievers—and winners. If you want to find them, just watch the World Series. Or simply read about New York Yankee great Lou Gehrig; Ted Williams, "the Splendid Splinter" of the Boston Red Sox; or the Dodgers' strikeout king Sandy Koufax.

A pitcher *should* be able to win a lot of ballgames with a 98-miles-per-hour fastball. But what about the pitcher who wins 20 games a year with a fastball so slow that you can catch it with your teeth? Bob Feller of the Cleveland Indians got into the Hall of Fame with a blazing fastball that glowed in the dark. National League star Grover Cleveland Alexander got there with a pitch that took considerably longer to reach the plate; but when it did arrive, the pitch was exactly where Alexander wanted it to be—and the last place the batter expected it to be.

There are probably more players with exceptional ability who didn't make it to the major leagues than there are who did. A number of great hitters, bored with fielding practice, had to be dropped from their team because their home-run production didn't make up for their lapses in the field. And then there are players like Brooks Robinson of the Baltimore Orioles, who made himself into a human vacuum cleaner at third base because he knew that working hard to become an expert fielder would win him a job in the big leagues.

A star is not something that flashes through the sky. That's a comet. Or a meteor. A star is something you can steer ships by. It stays in place and gives off a steady glow; it is fixed, permanent. A star works at being a star.

And that's how you tell a star in baseball. He shows up night after night and takes pride in how brightly he shines. He's Willie Mays running so hard his hat keeps falling off; Ty Cobb sliding to stretch a single into a double; Lou Gehrig, after being fooled in his first two at-bats, belting the next pitch off the light tower because he's taken the time to study the pitcher. Stars never take themselves for granted. That's why they're stars.

# 1

# PLAYING TO WIN

**D**uring the final month of the 1907 major league season, the American League pennant race was being called "the greatest struggle in the history of baseball." Half of the league's eight teams—the Detroit Tigers, Philadelphia Athletics, Chicago White Sox, and Cleveland Indians—were battling for first place. Only a few games separated the four clubs in the standings.

The Tigers were scratching and clawing for every victory when they faced the New York Highlanders (since renamed the New York Yankees) on a September afternoon in New York City. After eight innings, the two teams were locked in a scoreless duel.

Ty Cobb, Detroit's 20-year-old center fielder, opened the ninth inning by reaching first base. He dashed for second as the next batter swung at a pitch and missed. The catcher's throw was a little wide of the bag, and the ball bounced off the second baseman's glove, rolling a few feet away. Cobb slid safely into the base, popped up quickly, and raced for third. The crowd roared, certain that he would be thrown out by a mile.

*In addition to posting the highest career batting average of all time, Ty Cobb was one of the most daring baserunners ever to lace up a pair of spikes.*

The second baseman's throw would indeed have beaten Cobb easily to third. But the clever baserunner hurled his body into the ball's path. The baseball hit him in the back and bounced harmlessly away.

Two outs later, Cobb was still on third. When the next batter came up and the pitcher went into his windup, Cobb dashed halfway toward home plate, trying to distract the hurler. During the next windup, Cobb streaked for home and did not stop. The batter tapped the ball back to the rattled pitcher, who fumbled it and threw low to first base. The batter was safe. Meanwhile, Cobb scored what proved to be the winning run. In just his third major league season, the young player had introduced a new way to win games: make the opposing players beat themselves by getting on their nerves and forcing them to make mistakes.

The following afternoon, Cobb was on first base when a batter laid down a sacrifice bunt. Cobb ran to second as the bunted ball was fielded and thrown to Hal Chase, one of the best-fielding first basemen in the game. Chase made the putout at first base, then relaxed for a moment. He was amazed to see that Cobb had not stopped at second but had rounded the bag and was on his way to third.

In his eagerness to get Cobb out, Chase hurried his throw, and the ball sailed wide of third. With the throw pulling the third baseman off the bag, Cobb realized that the fielder would have to spin around, straighten up his body, and remove the ball from his glove before he could fire it home. So the swift runner kept right on going, and he slid across home plate just ahead of the catcher's tag. Cobb had scored from first base on a cleanly fielded sacrifice bunt!

Even those people who saw the play had a hard time believing it had happened. The New York players were stunned. Each of them swore that Cobb would not get away with a play like that ever again.

Ty Cobb was not one to back down from a challenge. The next day, he was quiet until the seventh inning, when he reached first base. The New Yorkers were on edge, waiting for him to pull some kind of stunt. When the next batter bunted, the fielder bobbled the ball. Cobb sped all the way to third, sliding in safely under the throw.

The third baseman, George Moriarty, got so mad he jumped up and down and slammed the ball to the ground. As it bounced high in the air, Cobb leaped up from the ground and raced for home. By the time the ball came down and Moriarty could grab and throw it, Cobb was dusting himself off from his slide across home plate.

Cobb continued to bewilder opposing players as the season entered its last week. The first-place Tigers held a slim lead over the Athletics on September 27 as the two teams met for a doubleheader. Although the Philadelphia ballpark seated only 18,000 people, a crowd of 30,000 crushed into the stadium that day. Many of the spectators stood in the outfield behind restraining ropes.

The Athletics led after five innings, 7–1, behind their ace left-hander, Rube Waddell. The Tigers fought back, however, and by the ninth inning they trailed 8–6. Cobb came to bat with a man on first.

Waddell, a future Hall of Famer, believed that Cobb's weakness as a hitter was an inside fastball, so he threw one. Cobb paid no attention

*Hall of Fame pitcher Rube Waddell ranks among the lifetime leaders in strikeouts, yet he had little success in striking out Cobb. Very few hurlers whiffed him, in fact; Cobb fanned just 357 times in 24 seasons.*

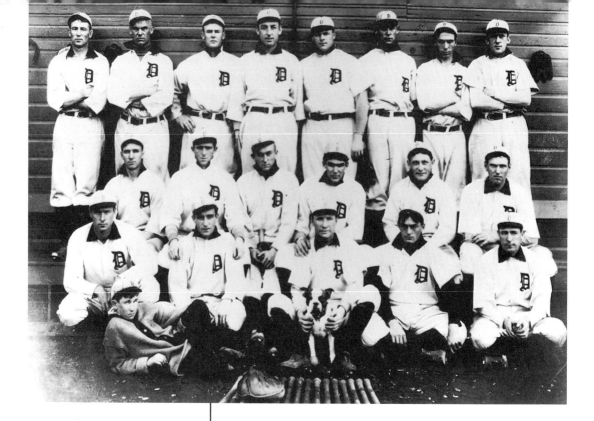

*In 1907, when the Detroit Tigers won the first of three straight American League pennants, Cobb (seated in the middle row, third from left) played his first full season with the ballclub.*

to the pitch; he just looked away. It went for strike one.

"I figure he's looking for a certain pitch," Waddell said later. "I see my chance to cross him up. I says to myself, I'll feed this cuckoo one in the same spot and get him in a hole, then let him guess on what's coming. I throws another for the inside corner and . . . this Cobb, who didn't seem to have noticed the first one, steps back . . . takes a toehold and swings. I guess the ball's going yet."

Cobb's home run tied the game. The score stayed tied through 17 innings, until it became too dark to play. Cobb would play in more than 3,000 games, but he said that none gave him as many thrills as that one. The Tigers left town in first place and held on to win the pennant, the team's first one ever.

After the game, Waddell asked Cobb why he had ignored the first fastball but was all set for the next one. Did he steal the catcher's sign to the pitcher?

Cobb told Waddell, "I figured if I let the first one pass and make out I don't notice it and am looking for something else, you'll try to cross me up and shoot the next one over the same spot. I feel so sure, when the ball leaves your hand I jump back, take a toehold and swing."

"Kid," said Waddell, "you had me doped a hundred percent right."

For the next 21 years, Cobb doped just about everybody a hundred percent right on the field. Using his intelligence to gain an edge over his opponents, he proved to be as much a genius in his field as the inventor Thomas Edison and the automobile manufacturer Henry Ford were in theirs. Cobb's brains, speed, and daring helped him post a .367 lifetime batting average, the highest of all time.

Yet Ty Cobb was much more than a smart and talented ballplayer. He was also the fiercest, most intensely driven competitor any sport has ever seen. He could endure anything except failure or defeat. He is considered the greatest player in baseball history. But because he always played to win at all costs, he was also called the dirtiest, meanest, most hated man who ever wore spikes.

# 2
# THE BASEBALL BUG

Tyrus Raymond Cobb was born on December 18, 1886, in the northeast corner of Georgia, in a farming valley called the Narrows. About 50 people lived in the valley, and a number of them had been Confederate officers during the Civil War. These former soldiers never stopped believing in the nobility of their cause, even though it had been more than 20 years since the South had lost the war. Ty grew up listening to tales of the rebels' heroics in the Civil War and took pride in his southern heritage.

The Cobbs of Georgia already boasted an illustrious heritage by the time Ty entered the world. Among his ancestors were several Civil War generals and Confederate statesmen. One of them, Howell Cobb, was a Speaker of the U.S. House of Representatives who later became governor of Georgia.

Ty's father, William H. Cobb, had already begun to establish his own place on the family tree. He was an educated man who taught in a one-room school in the valley. Most people

*The future Hall of Famer (left) at about the age of 12, with his sister, Florence, and brother, Paul.*

15

called him Professor. He was stern and demanding, and he had a way of making nearly everyone try to impress him. He married Amanda Chitwood, a Confederate captain's daughter, when he was in his early twenties and she was only 12 years old. Three years later, Ty was born, followed in 1888 by a brother, Paul, and a sister, Florence, in 1892.

Ty was a terror from an early age. Stubborn and hot-tempered, he could think quicker and run faster than the other children in the Narrows. But he could not stand to lose at anything. He had to be the best at running races, throwing rocks, and climbing trees. When he was in the fifth grade, he beat up a classmate after the boy missed a word in a spelling bee and allowed the girls' team to win.

Baseball proved to be a natural outlet for Ty's competitive spirit. He delighted in batting against a pitcher and in challenging the fielders whenever he was on the basepaths. To his way of thinking, baseball was more of an individual contest than a team sport.

Baseball was the most popular sport in the United States even back when Ty was growing up. Almost every town had an amateur ballclub, and the teams in neighboring towns often developed rivalries. In the 1890s, the Cobbs moved to a farm near the town of Royston, which had two clubs. One team was called the Royston Rompers, for boys aged 12 to 14, and Ty became the shortstop.

One Saturday, the local men's team, the Royston Reds, needed a shortstop and asked Ty to play for them. The fact that the other players were much older than he was did not bother young Ty. He proudly put on the club's bright-

A youthful Cobb (front row, far left) poses with the first team he ever played for, the Royston Reds. The fact that the other players were much older than he was did not seem to bother Ty at all.

red uniform, then collected three hits and handled eight chances in the field without an error. He later said he got a tingling sensation when he stroked his first hit with the Reds, and it was this feeling that helped convince him to choose a career in athletics.

The Reds soon had a big game at Elberton, 20 miles away. Ty had to plow the cornfield on the family farm that day, but the Reds' manager talked Professor Cobb into letting Ty play. He got three hits and drove in the winning run. In another game, he saved a victory with a diving catch in the outfield and felt the thrill of being cheered by a big crowd for the first time.

Ty was definitely making great strides as a player. He had made his first baseball by winding cord around a rubber ball, and he had sewed two ragged pieces of leather together for a glove.

But now that he had made up his mind to continue playing for the Reds, he felt that he needed a better glove. He saw a beauty in a store in town, but he did not have any money. His father's library, however, was filled with handsome leather-bound books that looked very expensive. Ty figured a few of them would never be missed, so he "borrowed" them and traded them for the glove.

Unfortunately for Ty, Professor Cobb noticed the missing books and called his son into the study, then closed the door behind them. "Let us draw the curtain of mercy over that scene," Ty wrote later. "I wasn't able to forget what happened there for many, many months."

Ty's father believed that baseball was a waste of time. There were more important things to do, such as plowing and seeding the fields of the family farm. Professor Cobb also expected his eldest son to be studious and well behaved in school. Ty was neither. He hated anything that kept him from playing baseball.

Nevertheless, Professor Cobb's standing as a scholar and Royston's leading citizen put pressure on Ty. The teacher had recently become the town's mayor and had started a weekly newspaper. In time, he would become a state senator, help establish the state's first public school system, and win election as Franklin County's first school commissioner.

Ty did not want to let his father down. He felt driven to prove himself. Yet he was not sure that he wanted to go to college, and he was certainly not interested in attending a military school, even if it was the U.S. Military Academy at West Point, New York, or the U.S. Naval Academy at Annapolis, Maryland.

As Ty looked around for a career, he realized that he did not want to become a lawyer. Professor Cobb arranged for Ty to meet with a well-known attorney and look over a few law books. But the teenager found them boring.

Ty thought he might like to become a surgeon, so he began to accompany the local doctor as he made his rounds. One night, a boy was shot in the stomach, and Ty went with Doctor Moss to the youngster's home. The doctor handed Ty a cloth and a bottle of chloroform to use in putting the boy to sleep before they operated on him. Next, the physician cut open the boy's stomach. Unable to find the bullet in the pale light of an oil lamp, Doctor Ross asked Ty to poke around in the intestines for the piece of metal. He had no luck, either.

The sight of blood did not bother Ty. In fact, he would see plenty of it from spike wounds. But the experience helped him realize that he was not interested in pursuing a medical career.

In the spring of 1903, Ty tried to become more enthusiastic about his farm chores. He worked so hard at growing cotton that he got a job with a cotton dealer. He soon learned everything about how cotton was ginned, baled, graded, and marketed. Ty often discussed the cotton business with his father, and their conversations soon helped them form a closer bond.

But baseball remained the only thing Ty truly liked. He even enjoyed making his own bats. Aided by a friend whose father built coffins, Ty got hold of high-quality ash wood and the tools needed to make the bats.

It seems that as much as Ty's father wanted his son to shake the baseball bug, the 17-year-old could not do it.

*Cobb (top row, third from right) as a minor leaguer with the Augusta Tourists in 1905, shortly before the Georgia-based ballclub sold his contract to the Detroit Tigers.*

# 3

# "DON'T COME HOME A FAILURE"

In early 1904, Ty Cobb learned about a new minor league being formed. Known as the South Atlantic ("Sally") League, it had six teams located in three states: Georgia, Florida, and South Carolina. Cobb wrote a letter to each ballclub and asked for a tryout. The manager of the Augusta, Georgia, team invited him to spring training and promised the 17-year-old a salary of $50 a month if he made the roster.

Cobb told his mother about the Augusta Tourists' offer right away. But the teenager waited until the evening before he was to leave town to break the news to his father. Professor Cobb spent most of that night lecturing his son, warning him that most ballplayers were gamblers and drunks—which in the early 1900s was true—and that Ty was risking his future by heading off to play baseball. The young man did not argue. All he could say was, "I just have to go."

"Get it out of your system," Ty's father said at last. And then the always practical professor proceeded to write out a half dozen checks for $15 each, to be used for living expenses. He put a different date on each check so his son could not cash them—and spend the $90—all at once.

The following morning, the budding young ballplayer took his favorite bat and a change of clothes and started out on an all-day train trip that took him just 85 miles from home. The city of Augusta, however, was a world away from the small town of Royston. Forty thousand people lived in this busy hive of industry.

Cobb went all-out from the first day of workouts at Augusta's Warren Park. The older players thought he cut a comical figure as he ran wild in his bright-red Royston uniform. Nobody took him seriously, and he failed to play in any of the team's exhibition games.

But as luck would have it, on the day that the Sally League season opened, one of the Tourists' players failed to show up. Cobb was placed on the team's roster and was given the chance to start in center field. He hit a single and a double, and after the game he was feeling puffed up with confidence. The absent player showed up two days later, however, which prompted the manager to call Cobb over and tell him he was being released.

Angry, confused, and heartsick, Cobb went back to his hotel room. There, another player who had just been let go by the Tourists told him about a semipro team in Alabama that was looking for ballplayers.

"I don't know," Cobb said. "When I left home my father told me to come down here and get all this baseball out of my system and then come home and go to college. I'll have to talk to him first." Dreading what his father would say, Ty went to the local telephone office and called home.

"What are you going to do now?" Professor Cobb asked.

"Well, you see," Ty mumbled, "there is this job open over in Anniston, Alabama."

To Ty's surprise, his father said, "Go after it. And I want to tell you one other thing. Don't come home a failure."

Ty Cobb never forgot his father's words. "In giving me his blessing," the ballplayer said later, "his sanction of my quest for success in my hour of defeat, my father put more determination in me than he ever knew. I had the shivers when I hung up."

Ignited by his intense desire to make good, Cobb burned up the league at Anniston, hitting and running the bases like blazes. He was not the fastest man on the team, but he had studied the art of sprinting and getting a quick start. In the years that followed, he even put lead weights in his shoes during spring training to strengthen his legs and make them feel lighter and swifter in games.

Cobb also discovered that if he swung three bats while waiting his turn at bat, then cast two of them aside, the one he swung at the plate seemed light as a feather. He was probably the first player to practice that. In addition, he learned to control his bat exceptionally well by holding his bottom hand a few inches from the knob and spreading his hands apart on the handle. This unique grip enabled him to hit the ball to any spot he aimed for. It proved so successful, in fact, that he never changed his batting style.

Eager to be noticed, Cobb wrote letters and postcards and sent telegrams to Grantland Rice, the sports editor of the *Atlanta Journal.* Each of

*"The blackest of days" in Cobb's life was August 9, 1905, when he received word that his mother, Amanda (opposite page), had just shot and killed his father, William (above), as he tried to enter their house through a bedroom window. She was charged with voluntary manslaughter, but a jury found her not guilty in her trial the following spring.*

these communications praised a young star named Cobb and detailed his phenomenal feats in every game. To give the impression that a lot of people were mounting this publicity campaign, Cobb altered his handwriting on each letter and signed every one with a different name.

Nothing came of it for weeks. Then one day Cobb saw this brief item in the Atlanta newspaper: "Rumors have reached Atlanta from numerous sources that over in Alabama there's a young fellow named Cobb who seems to be showing an unusual amount of talent." Many years later, Cobb confessed to Rice that he alone had been the "numerous sources."

"Why did you do it?" Rice asked.

"I was in a hurry," Cobb told him.

Apparently, Rice's words of praise pleased Professor Cobb immensely. He carried the clipping around and showed it proudly to his friends. Ty did not learn about his father's actions, however, until a few years later.

In August 1904, the Augusta Tourists needed an outfielder and asked Cobb to return to the club. After making sure that the manager who had fired him was no longer with the team, Cobb agreed. He finished the season with a .237 batting average in 35 games and returned home with $200 in his pockets. Unfortunately, the Tourists failed to promise him that he would be invited back in 1905.

Cobb spent the winter walking in the woods, hunting, and sowing the winter wheat crop. All the while, he wondered if he should enter the University of Georgia and forget about baseball. But when the Tourists agreed to pay him $90 a month for the upcoming season, he stopped thinking about attending school.

Returning to Augusta in the spring, Cobb got a chance to show off his playing style to the Detroit Tigers, who trained at Warren Park along with the Tourists. The big leaguers were amused by the baserunning antics of the 18-year-old Cobb. "He's the craziest ballplayer I ever saw," the Tigers' second baseman laughed. Still, he was impressed by the teenager's hitting ability.

Cobb was Augusta's starting left fielder when the season opened. He began slowly, as did the entire team. Pretty soon, it seemed that nobody on the ballclub cared if a game was won or lost—not even Cobb. One day, he brought a bag of popcorn to his position in the outfield. When a fly ball was hit his way, he was more concerned with not spilling any popcorn than with catching the ball, and he missed it. George Leidy, who had just become the team's manager, was not pleased.

That night, Leidy invited Cobb to go with him to an amusement park. During the trolley ride to the park site, Leidy talked about the bright future Cobb had in baseball if he applied himself. The manager spoke to the teenager about the grand life of a major leaguer: the wonderful sights of the big cities, the large sums of money to be earned, the fame and success to be achieved.

Leidy and Cobb held similar conversations on many other nights. And every morning, the manager worked with the left-handed batter on improving his hitting, bunting, and baserunning skills. Cobb soon became the star of the Sally League.

It was not easy to tell that Cobb was a ballplayer simply by looking at him. While riding on a train one day, the spindly teenager met a fat youth named Oliver Hardy. When Cobb said he was a baseball player, the heavy lad laughed.

"What are you, the batboy?"

"Batboy!" Cobb yelled. "Come out to the game and I'll show you what I am."

His pride stung, Cobb collected four hits, including a home run, and stole two bases. His performance surely brought a smile to the face of Oliver Hardy, who knew a thing or two about smiles. Teaming up with Stan Laurel years later, he became one of the most famous comedians in the world.

Stories told about famous people often become added to or altered until they bear little resemblance to the truth. Still, they usually illustrate something about the person who is the star of the story. So it is with stories about Ty Cobb, such as the one about him and his roommate, pitcher Nap Rucker, in 1905.

Because there were no showers at Warren Park, the players changed at the boardinghouse where they lived. One day, Rucker reached the room first and got into the bathtub. When Cobb found the bathroom occupied, he banged loudly on the door and shouted, "I take my bath first!" When Cobb finally calmed down, he said, "Try to understand, Nap. I got sore when you beat me to the bathtub. I have to be first in everything."

By midsummer in 1905, major league scouts were studying Cobb's every move. It looked as if he would soon be able to tell his father that he had been promoted to the big leagues. But before the day arrived, Cobb received the news that his father had been shot and killed.

In the early hours of August 9, Amanda Cobb was asleep in bed when she was awakened by a sound on the porch roof. Someone was trying to enter the bedroom through one of the windows. Thinking it was a burglar, she reached for a nearby shotgun and fired at the shadowy figure. The blast killed the man, who turned out to be Professor Cobb.

Devastated, Ty made the sad journey home for his father's funeral. The day after Professor Cobb was buried, Ty's mother was arrested and charged with voluntary manslaughter. She was soon released on bail; and in her trial the following spring, the jury found her not guilty.

All Cobb could do to forget about this horrible incident was to concentrate on baseball. He returned to the Tourists a week after the shooting. Three days later, the 18-year-old was told that he was being sent to the major leagues. He had been sold to the Detroit Tigers for $750. "I only thought," Cobb recalled, "Father won't know it."

# 4

# THE HOT-
# TEMPERED ROOKIE

*Cobb stands at the plate at Augusta's Warren Park in 1906 during his first spring training as a member of the Detroit Tigers. He always choked up on the handle to give himself extra control of the bat.*

On August 30, 1905, after three days and nights on a train, 18-year-old Ty Cobb awoke in the biggest city he had ever seen. Located on a river that flows into Lake Erie, Detroit was one of the fastest growing cities in the United States. It was a big manufacturing center and a busy port for shipping lumber and iron ore. And the city would soon become the center of the nation's automobile industry.

As Cobb walked to the Detroit Tigers' ballpark on streets made of cedar blocks, he listened to the din of factory whistles and trolley bells and clattering horse-drawn carts. The accents of Irish and German immigrants he heard on the street sounded strange to the teenager, who had never before been in the North.

Bennett Park was a rickety wooden grandstand with only 8,000 seats, but it seemed huge to Cobb. The Tigers' regular center fielder was hurt, and the Detroit manager immediately put Cobb in the lineup, batting him fifth. The first big league pitcher he faced was the New York Highlanders' Jack Chesbro, who had won 41 games the previous year. That total did not scare

*Jack Chesbro of the New York Highlanders, who set a modern-day record by winning 41 games in 1904, was the first pitcher Cobb batted against in the major leagues. The rookie lashed a double to left-center field off the spit-balling right-hander for the first of his 4,191 career base hits.*

Cobb. In his first time at bat, he lashed a double and drove in a run.

Cobb marveled at the way baseball was played in the big leagues, with speed and skill and fiery spirit. The players appeared to be older, tougher, and smarter than any he had ever seen.

The next day, the big leaguers initiated Cobb into their world. After one of the two singles he hit that afternoon, he tried to steal second base by sliding headfirst. The shortstop, Kid Elberfeld, took the catcher's throw and tagged out Cobb. At the same time, Elberfeld jammed his knee against the rookie's neck and ground his face into the dirt. Sliding headlong was considered "bush league," and Cobb, rising from the ground with a scraped nose, learned it could also be dangerous. He rarely slid headfirst after this incident.

For the most part, Cobb's dashing style made a good impression on the fans. But he was awkward and made mistakes. He still had a lot to learn, and so he practiced a lot.

Cobb spent long hours chasing after fly balls. He dug up some dirt and made a sliding pit, where he practiced sliding until his legs and hips were scraped raw and bleeding. He developed nine different ways to slide, never giving an opposing player more than a toe or finger to tag. He studied pitchers, catchers, and fielders until he knew all their movements, habits, and facial expressions.

If a pitcher gave him trouble, Cobb did not rest until he had figured out how to solve the puzzle. For a long time, a left-hander, Doc White, got him out with sharp curveballs. Cobb studied and studied, then decided that if he moved back a few feet in the batter's box, he would have an extra split second to hit the ball as it dropped through the strike zone. He had no more trouble with White after that.

Cobb was not the best natural hitter or fielder or the fastest runner. But he became the greatest player in the game because he had the quickest-working brain and the strongest desire to win. He knew his opponents' strengths and weaknesses and had the courage and daring to take advantage of them. He outthought them, did the unexpected, and kept everybody on edge.

Sometimes it looked as if Cobb was doing something dumb. But it was part of his plan to catch the other team off guard another time. There were a few times, however, when his recklessness resulted in his stealing a base when there was a baserunner already on it.

Cobb played in 41 games in 1905 and posted a .240 batting average. It was the only time he hit below .300 in his major league career.

The older players mostly ignored Cobb that first year, which was the way they usually treated late-season rookies. But the next spring was another story. Cobb's arrival at the 1906 spring training camp in Augusta began what he later called his "most miserable and humiliating experience."

There are several reasons why some of the Tigers ganged up on Cobb and tried to drive him off the team. Mainly, they saw him as a threat to take a job from one of their pals. He was a southerner, and all the other players were from the North. Also, Cobb was proud and sensitive and hardly had any sense of humor. When the veterans gave him the usual hazing that rookies got, or kidded him about the South losing the Civil War, it made him fighting mad.

*Cobb sends the dirt flying as he slides safely into third base against the New York Highlanders at New York City's Hilltop Grounds in 1909. Later that year, St. Louis Browns manager Jimmy McAleer called him "the greatest piece of baseball machinery that ever stepped on the diamond."*

The more Cobb snarled back or put up his fists, the more his teammates poured it on. They locked him out of the only bathroom in the hotel after practice. They threw spitballs at him. They tore his clothes and sawed his favorite home-made bats in half. The other players refused to back him up in the outfield, so he had to chase down balls that got by him.

Cobb hated his teammates, and they hated him. Although they came to respect him as a player, some of the Tigers never shook Cobb's hand or spoke to him ever again. In fact, he became so wary of the other players that he began to carry a pistol with him.

There were a few players who tried to be friendly to Cobb, but he had the personality of a bear with a toothache. Some people go through life with a chip on their shoulder; Ty Cobb carried a lumberyard. He believed in the proverb: "Beware of entrance to a quarrel but once you are in it, let the other side watch out for you." To Cobb, life seemed to be one long quarrel. Over the years, he got into shouting and shoving matches with waitresses, parking-lot attendants, clubhouse boys, shopkeepers, laborers, and customs officials. He fought with players on and off the field, and he once battled an umpire under the grandstand while players and fans watched.

Bitter and lonely, Cobb ate by himself and roomed alone, using his free time to think of ways to fool the other team and get an edge on his foes. The rough treatment he suffered only added to his desire to outperform everyone.

On the way north from spring training in 1906, Cobb's tonsils became infected. By the time the Tigers reached Toledo, Ohio, he could hardly swallow. Afraid that the manager would release him if he was sick, Cobb called the hotel doctor.

Germany Schaefer, one of the few teammates who got along well with Cobb, held down the 19-year-old in a chair. Then the physician, without using any anesthesia to deaden the pain, began to cut out the ballplayer's swollen tonsils. With Cobb taking time out to recover from the pain and loss of blood, the brutal operation took two days for the doctor to finish. Cobb later heard that the physician had been committed to an insane asylum.

Cobb stole 23 bases in 97 games and batted .320—the highest average on the team that year. He was a peach of a player, and one writer aptly nicknamed him the Georgia Peach.

Yet Cobb was more like a tiger with spikes. He drove himself without letup and drove everybody else crazy trying to stop him. He made himself the best. But he paid a heavy price for it.

His spikes flying high, Cobb tries to avoid a tag by
Frank ("Home Run") Baker and winds up spiking the
Philadelphia Athletics third baseman on the arm. Taking
place on August 24, 1909, this incident prompted
American League president Ban Johnson to state that
Cobb "must stop this sort of playing or he will have to
quit the game."

# FLASHING SPIKES

**O**ne of the best things that happened to Ty Cobb was the naming of Hugh Jennings as the Detroit Tigers manager in 1907. A red-haired, freckled fellow with a big grin, Jennings was a noisy leader. Whenever he was coaching at third base, he would pull up grass by the handful and fling it in the air, whistling shrilly and shouting "Ee-yah" and "Attaboy" to keep his players fired up. He appreciated Cobb's abilities and allowed him to run whenever he wanted and to bunt or hit away as he saw fit.

To Cobb, baseball was a war, the pitcher was the enemy, and anybody who got in the way was an obstacle to be eliminated. If they threw at his head, stepped on his toes, smacked him in the face with the ball, or threatened to break his legs, what was he supposed to do? "If I'd been meek and submissive and hadn't fought back, the world never would have heard of Ty Cobb," he said.

Nobody had ever run the bases the way Cobb did, so his style caught everyone by surprise. He served notice that anyone blocking a base or trying to tag him was in danger of being spiked.

*Detroit Tigers manager Hugh ("Ee-yah") Jennings offers encouragement to his players from the third-base coach's box. Cobb's skipper for 14 seasons, Jennings let his star player try to steal a base whenever he wanted.*

It was nothing personal—just get out of my way, he warned. "The rules say a baseline belongs to me."

The players whose legs and arms were sliced by his spikes did not see it that way. They called Cobb a dirty player. Stories were invented that he often sat on the bench gleefully sharpening his spikes with a file (which he did just once, as a joke). Stories are still written today that portray him as a man who would spike his own mother to reach a base.

Cobb later complained that history never told the whole story. "They wrote how I'd tear into home plate with my spikes high as if I intended to cut the catcher in half," he said. "What they didn't mention was that the catcher would put his mask in front of the plate and the bat, too, if he had time to reach it. Paul Krichell of the Browns did that once too often. I slid in high, scissored him between my legs, a bone snapped in his shoulder and the guy never caught another ball game in his life."

Cobb's reputation intimidated infielders and made them nervous and less willing to hang in there when they saw him bearing down on them. Jennings said, "He was the most fearless player I have ever known. He had half the American League players scared stiff." One pitcher covering home plate ran away when Cobb started sliding toward him.

Cobb was reckless and enjoyed doing the unexpected. He would go from first to third on an infield out, score from second on a fly ball, and take an extra base while a fielder held the ball and watched him. "Make them keep throwing the ball," he said. "Sooner or later someone is sure to make a wild throw."

Cobb stole second, third, and home in one inning three times in his career. Veteran shortstop Everett Scott said, "He is the only man in baseball who ever gave me a thrill. I'll never see a more fascinating picture than he made tearing down the baseline. He was a cyclone, a tornado, a typhoon all rolled into one."

Branch Rickey, who managed the rival St. Louis Browns during the middle years of Cobb's career, recalled, "One day he was on first base against us. The pitcher threw over to first and Cobb got back in time. But as the first baseman lobbed the ball back to the pitcher, Cobb was off in a flash streaking for second. The pitcher hurried his throw and it went into center field. Cobb popped to his feet and headed for third. The throw had him beaten, but the third baseman dropped the ball. Cobb slid for the ball and kicked it into the dugout, then got up and jogged home with the winning run. It was a clear case of interference, but the umpires said it must have been an accident. They could not believe that any player could perform such a stunt on purpose."

In 1907, Cobb's 212 hits, 49 stolen bases, 116 runs batted in, and .350 batting average led the American League in each category, and the Tigers won the first of three straight pennants. Each race was a close one that went down to the closing days of the season. Detroit finished on top in 1907 by one-and-a-half games and in 1908 by half a game.

In 1909, the Tigers were again battling the Athletics as the two teams opened a big series in Philadelphia on August 24. Early in the game, Cobb slid into third base as Frank ("Home Run") Baker reached to tag him. Cobb's spikes opened

*Cobb chats with Cleveland Indians star Shoeless Joe Jackson before a game in 1912. The previous year, Cobb had beat out Jackson in the race for the American League batting title by posting a career-high .420 average.*

a slight cut on Baker's arm. Tape was put over the wound, and Baker stayed in the game.

The fans howled at Cobb, however, and newspaper headlines screamed that he was a dirty player who had intentionally slashed Baker to shreds. Cobb should be kicked out of baseball, the papers said.

That same night, a big crowd in an ugly mood gathered outside Cobb's hotel. Determined to take his nightly walk, he passed through the yelling mob unharmed. He received letters, phone calls, and telegrams that threatened to harm him if he played again.

The next day, Cobb was escorted to the ballpark by policemen on motorcycles. The lawmen formed a solid wall of blue coats between the Tigers center fielder and the overflow crowd that stood behind ropes in the outfield. He was loudly booed, but he was not hurt by anyone.

Cobb never forgave the writers who had fanned the flames of hatred with their attacks on him. He always maintained that Baker had been out of position when he was cut. Baker, in fact, never accused Cobb of being a dirty player or of cutting him on purpose.

Thanks largely to Cobb and his teammates Donie Bush, Sam Crawford, George Mullin, and Ed Willett, Detroit won the 1909 pennant by three-and-a-half games. Despite their heavy-hitting lineup, the Tigers lost their third straight World Series. Most of the time, Cobb was not a World Series hero. He batted only .200 in the 1907 Series against the Chicago Cubs. He hit .368 in the Series the following year against the same team. But in 1909 he posted a meager .231 batting average in the seven-game Series against the Pittsburgh Pirates.

And yet for nine straight years, from 1907 through 1915, Cobb led the American League in batting. He was also the league's leading hitter from 1917 through 1919, which meant that he won an amazing 12 batting titles in 13 years. He batted over .400 in two of those seasons— 1911 (.420) and 1912 (.410)—and also hit .401 in 1922.

Even though Cobb posted a career-high .420 average in 1911, he might have lost the batting title if he had not employed some of his legendary tactics. Shoeless Joe Jackson, a young outfielder with the Cleveland Indians and a friendly fellow southerner, was leading Cobb by nine points in the batting race when the two ballclubs met near the end of the season. On the field before the first game, Jackson asked Cobb, "How you been, Ty?"

Cobb looked the other way and did not answer. Jackson was puzzled.

"What's the matter, Ty?"

"Get away from me," Cobb snarled.

Throughout the six-game series, Jackson kept asking, "What's wrong, Ty?" But Cobb never answered. His mind was fixed on getting base hits.

Meanwhile, Jackson seemed to become upset by Cobb's silence. In any event, Cobb fattened up his batting average while Jackson went into a slump.

When the last game of the series was over, Cobb walked over to Jackson and said with a big smile, "Hello, Joe, how's your health?" The Tigers center fielder wound up beating Jackson in the batting race by 12 points.

"It helps," Cobb said later, "if you help them beat themselves."

# 6

# WEALTHY, FAMOUS, AND LONELY

On August 3, 1908, Ty Cobb left the Detroit Tigers for a week and returned to Georgia to marry 17-year-old Charlie Lombard. The 21-year-old ballplayer had gone home in the middle of a close pennant race, without telling anyone in the ballclub's front office. That he could suddenly leave the team without getting into trouble was proof that he had become a very big star indeed.

The magazine *Sporting Life* later described Cobb's first wife as "a very patient little woman," and Charlie showed how patient she was right at the start of their marriage. During the wedding reception, which was held on August 6 in Augusta, she allowed her husband to carry around his favorite black bat. After all, it had helped him win his first batting championship.

Ty and Charlie's marriage lasted for 39 years. They had three sons—Tyrus, Jr., Herschel, and James—and two daughters, Shirley and Beverly. Cobb made sure that his children received a good education. In fact, he provided them with the best of everything. (He also supported his

*Cobb in 1915, when he won his ninth straight American League batting title. His 96 stolen bases that season also set a record that lasted for nearly half a century.*

mother and sister for many years.) Yet he was seldom at home. He traveled a lot during the baseball season. And each year after the major league season ended, he played in a winter league in California. Then he went golfing and hunting.

An avid sportsman, Cobb bred and trained hunting dogs all his life. "I've loved every one I ever owned," he said. "Dogs are better judges of people than people are of dogs. No man ever had a friend as honest or faithful as a dog. There is no truer companion . . . and a boy in the company of a dog is in good company."

Another of Cobb's hobbies was to drive racing cars; he loved to travel at high speeds almost as much as he liked to tear around the basepaths. He was especially thrilled in 1910, when his friend Barney Oldfield set a world speed record by driving an automobile at 131 miles per hour. Cobb decided to end his own racing career, however, when his own driving partner was killed in a race.

Because Cobb was left alone by his teammates, he did not go to saloons or pool halls, as many ballplayers did after a ballgame. Instead, he frequented the public rooms of the Pontchartrain Hotel in Detroit, where businessmen and promoters often gathered. Some of these men, such as Louis Chevrolet, Henry Ford, and Ransom Olds, would soon become the giants of the American automobile industry.

During Cobb's first few years with the Tigers, he did not have enough money to act on the investment tips he learned about in the public rooms. When he finally began to make investments, he used his knowledge of the cotton industry to make a lot of money. Before long,

*Back home in Georgia, Cobb poses for a family portrait with his first wife, Charlie, and two of their five children, Shirley and Tyrus, Jr.*

he was approaching business matters with the same enthusiasm that he showed when playing baseball.

Cobb invested his 1909 World Series check in copper mines, a move that paid off handsomely. He purchased stock in General Motors when it was formed; as the car company grew into a giant corporation, so did his investment. He bought real estate and owned an automobile dealership. Later on, he was persuaded to put money in a new company called Coca-Cola. He urged many players over the years to buy stock in the company, but very few had either the money or the courage to follow his good advice.

In the early 1900s, it was common for a star ballplayer to add to his salary by appearing in vaudeville shows and theatrical productions. In the winter of 1911, Cobb accepted the role of the football hero in the play *The College Widow*. But he did not like the grind of saying the same lines seven times a week and quit after two months. In 1916, he became an actor once more, starring in *Somewhere in Georgia*, a silent movie written by Grantland Rice. The motion picture did not make much money and was soon forgotten.

Cobb eventually became a millionaire and the wealthiest player in the game. In addition to making good business deals, he held out for more money from the Tigers each year. By 1914, he had become the highest-paid ballplayer, earning an annual salary of $15,000.

Cobb received other handsome rewards as well. In 1910, the Chalmers Automobile Company offered a new car to the American League batting champion. Cobb was a few points ahead of Cleveland's popular star, Nap Lajoie, on the last day of the season. The Indians closed out their schedule with two games at St. Louis, however, and the Browns hated Cobb so much that they wanted Lajoie to win the car. So they let the Cleveland second baseman beat out bunts all day.

Lajoie wound up the afternoon with eight hits, but Cobb still topped him, batting .385 to Lajoie's .384. Generously, the Chalmers Com-

*Cobb sits behind the wheel in one of his two Chalmers "30" automobiles. The first car was given to him in 1910 for winning the American League batting title; the second vehicle was his prize for being named the league's most valuable player in 1911.*

pany gave each ballplayer a car. The next year, Cobb received another car from Chalmers, this time for being named the American League's most valuable player.

Why did other players hate Cobb so much? He taunted them and made them look foolish. Sometimes he would fake a leg injury and roll on the ground in agony. After limping about painfully, he would steal a base on the next pitch. There were times when Cobb would steal second and the catcher would throw to *third* to stop him from running.

Awed by Cobb's daring style, baseball rooters booed him wherever he played. One day in 1912, a particularly foul-mouthed heckler rode Cobb so hard the ballplayer leaped into the seats and beat up the fan. He was suspended by the league for 10 days and fined $50, but the Tigers rallied around him. When the team moved on to Philadelphia, the ballplayers refused to take the field unless Cobb was reinstated. Rather than forfeit the game and pay a fine, Manager Hugh Jennings and his coaches rounded up some college and semipro players and put them in Detroit uniforms. The Athletics beat these Tigers, 24–2.

The next day, the American League president threatened to ban all the striking players from baseball for life unless they played. Cobb thanked his teammates for their support and urged them to end the strike, which they did.

It was clear that the more the fans rode Cobb, the harder he tried, so managers told their players to leave him alone. Cobb was afraid of nothing. He could dish it out, but he could take it, too. His legs were proof of that. They were covered with thick scars from his hips to his ankles.

*Four years after Cobb said, "I have observed that baseball is not unlike a war," he got a taste of the real thing. In 1918, with the United States engaged in World War I, he enlisted in the army and served in the same military outfit as National League star Christy Mathewson (left).*

Cobb made his own teammates as nervous as the opposition. If one of the Tigers missed a sign from the manager or made a mistake, Cobb had sharp words for him. He helped some players become better hitters, but he would push his advice on them even if they did not want it. At the same time, they appreciated his value to the team.

After Cobb had spent five years in the big leagues, experts said that he would soon burn himself out because he played so intensely every minute that he was on the field. But he took care of himself. During the season, he ate a lot of fruit and milk and eggs, but very little red meat. He strengthened his legs by walking many miles every winter. He suffered one serious knee injury, and he also weakened his arm while practicing pitching. But he generally avoided injuries, in part because he completely relaxed his body whenever he slid into a base.

Instead of burning out, Cobb continued to play at top speed. In 1909, he set an American League mark with 76 stolen bases. He established a new record in 1911, with 83. And in 1915 he stole 96 bases, a major league record that stood for 47 years. Cobb ended his career as baseball's all-time leading base stealer, until Rickey Henderson passed him in 1991.

In 1918, with the United States engaged in World War I, Cobb enlisted in the U.S. Army and became a captain in the Chemical Warfare Service. He served in the same outfit as future Hall of Fame pitcher Christy Mathewson. Both ballplayers were accidently poisoned with mustard gas during a training exercise, but the mishap had no lasting effects on Cobb. The war ended several months later and he was back in a Tigers uniform for the 1919 season.

Cobb did not mellow as he got older. He still had the disposition of a nest full of cranky hornets—and that was before something made him angry! On August 16, 1920, Ray Chapman, star shortstop of the Cleveland Indians, was killed when he was hit in the head by a pitch thrown by Carl Mays of the New York Yankees. Chapman was very popular, whereas Mays, who played the game the same way Cobb did, was not well liked. People said Mays had thrown at Chapman's head and should be run out of baseball.

Cobb was playing in Boston that day, and a New York reporter asked the Tigers star for his opinion on the matter. Although Cobb had tangled with Mays on several occasions, he told the sportswriter he had not seen the incident and therefore could not comment on it. Nevertheless, the reporter wrote that Cobb thought Mays should be barred from baseball, and several other newspapers picked up the story. The Yankees' fans read Cobb's reported comments and became furious with him.

When the Tigers arrived in New York City, Cobb had the flu and a 102-degree temperature. He should not have played, but he knew the New York crowd would call him yellow if he did not show up at the ballpark. Just before game time, he came out of the clubhouse, which was located beyond the outfield, and walked alone toward the infield. Thirty thousand fans immediately let loose a thunderous booing. Slowly, defiantly, Cobb walked to home plate, where he took off his cap and bowed to the crowd. Then he raised his arm toward the press section, indicating that the writers had falsely quoted him. It was Ty Cobb's nature never to back down from a challenge.

*Even though Cobb may have been the meanest player in the game, he would still take the time to delight a couple of young fans by autographing a baseball.*

# 7

# A FIGHTER TO THE END

At the end of the 1920 season, after 14 years at the helm of the Detroit Tigers, Hugh Jennings was tired and ready to retire. He urged Cobb to take his place, but Cobb did not want to be a manager. The Tigers owner kept after him, however, and Cobb finally agreed to pilot the team.

As a manager, Cobb did not spare the feelings of his players. If he did not like the way a pitcher was working, he would stand in center field, hold his nose, and wave his glove in the air. He was once so disgusted with a wild pitcher that he called time, walked to the mound, and took the ball from the hurler. Cobb threw a few strikes over the plate, then handed the ball to the pitcher and strolled back to the outfield.

Cobb improved the batting of some of his players, notably outfielder Harry Heilmann, who learned so well from the master that he won four batting championships, with averages between .393 and .403. Although the Tigers were the heaviest-hitting team in the majors under Cobb, he accused the ballclub's owner of not buying

*At New York City's Polo Grounds in 1920, a confident Babe Ruth appears to be lining up to take Cobb's place as the greatest player of all time. Because they represented very different approaches to how the game should be played, the two stars remained bitter rivals for nearly a decade. By the mid-1920s, however, they had begun to build a lasting friendship.*

the players a team needed to win. One second-place finish was the best he could do in six years as a manager.

The added responsibility did not affect Cobb's own performance. In 1924, he reached the 200-hit mark for the ninth time, which set a major league record. He wound up his career with 4,191 hits overall, a mark that stood for nearly 60 years.

As a ballplayer, Cobb hardly ever gave umpires any trouble. He never complained or showed them up, and they often gave him the benefit of the doubt on a close play. But as a manager he argued loud and often.

Cobb was also a cruel and humorless bench jockey. He was especially sharp-tongued when riding the biggest stars, trying to get them angry and distracted in the hope that they would lose their concentration. He constantly needled Babe Ruth and Lou Gehrig, the two best-liked players in the game.

Cobb, for one, did not like how Ruth had changed the way baseball was played. The Babe had put an end to the era of low-scoring, strategic baseball—the type of game Cobb excelled at—in favor of the home run and the big inning. For 15 years, Cobb had been baseball's biggest star. But he lost that distinction when Ruth began to clout home runs.

Whenever sportswriters compared the two stars, they wrote about Cobb's bunts and singles versus Ruth's mighty blasts. That irritated Cobb. On May 5, 1925, while in St. Louis, he announced that if he tried, he could hit home runs as easily as Ruth did. "I'll show you something today," he promised. "I'm going for home runs for the first time in my career."

That afternoon, Cobb hit three balls out of the park, along with two singles and a double. His 16 total bases in one game set an American League record. The next day, he hit two more home runs, making him the first player in 40 years to hit five homers in two consecutive games.

In spite of this performance, Cobb had trouble with his eyes that year; a growth was clouding his vision. The following spring, he had the growth removed from both eyes.

Around the time of this operation, Cobb considered retiring from baseball. He had all the money he needed. He was nearing 40, and his body ached from April to September because he drove it so hard. And he could no longer dash around the bases like he had when he was younger.

Cobb did not know any other way to play the game; he had to shoot the works all the time. "I was like a steel spring," he said. "The slightest flaw will cause an overworked spring to fly apart, and then it is all done for."

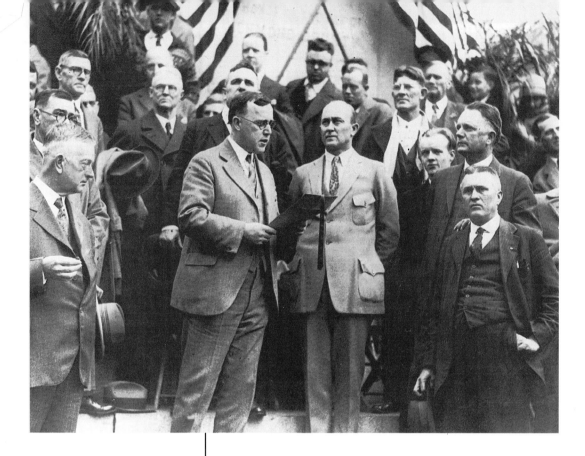

Cobb played in only 79 games in 1926. But he batted .339 and was less concerned about his own play than with his ballclub's performance. All through the season, he replayed in his mind the games his team lost and tried to figure out how to prevent those losses the next time. His mind never rested.

In November 1926, Cobb and Tris Speaker, the Cleveland manager, both resigned suddenly from their posts. The next month, Baseball Commissioner Kenesaw Mountain Landis released documents stating that Dutch Leonard, a former pitcher who held a grudge against Cobb and Speaker, had accused the two stars of fixing a game between their teams in 1919 and then betting on the outcome. Cobb and Speaker vehemently denied the charges, and they were cleared of any wrongdoing a few months later. Nevertheless, the events surrounding the incident had pressured them into resigning, and the scandal continued to make headlines for weeks afterward.

Once the episode was cleared up, Cobb received many offers from other teams. At age 40, he was tired and ready to quit, but he did not want to leave the game with a cloud over his name. Besides, baseball was his life. So he signed to play for one more year with the Philadelphia Athletics, whose manager, Connie Mack, Cobb admired and respected above all others. Also, the Athletics had a chance to win the 1927 pennant, and it had been 18 years since Cobb had been in a World Series.

At spring training in Ft. Myers, Florida, inventor Thomas A. Edison visited the Athletics' training camp and watched the players take batting practice. Cobb was on the mound when somebody invited the 80-year-old Edison to swing a bat. Cobb lobbed an easy toss to the elderly man, who swung and whacked a line drive that almost tore Cobb's ear off. Edison had studied and analyzed the batters' movements and then copied them. Cobb appreciated that.

Although Cobb had slowed down a lot, he still had a keen batting eye. On July 19, he collected the 4,000th hit of his career, making him the first player ever to reach that mark. He batted .357 for the season, but the Athletics finished the campaign in second place. The 1927 Yankees rolled over the league with what many consider to be baseball's greatest team ever.

After the season, Cobb agreed to play one more year with Philadelphia. He finished the 1928 season with a .323 batting average, but the

*Cobb stands alongside Frances Fairburn Cass in 1949, shortly before she became his second wife.*

Yankees edged out the Athletics in the last few days to win the pennant. Even so, Cobb said later that the two years he played for Connie Mack were the most enjoyable of his career.

Throughout Cobb's 24th and final big league season, he again seemed reluctant to drag his weary body away from the game. He was still hitting singles and daring outfielders to throw him out as he stretched them into doubles. One day in New York, Cobb stroked a base hit to right field, rounded first base, and raced for second. A strong throw came in to second baseman Tony Lazzeri, who was bent low in front of the bag. There was no way for Cobb to slide around him, so he leaped over Lazzeri's back and landed safely on the base.

A good loser might be defined as someone who can conceal his disappointment. A bad loser is one who cannot. Ty Cobb was the worst loser of all time. Personal defeat angered him, no matter what the game. There was no such thing as a friendly contest of golf or cards. He would look for any advantage to win a dollar, whether it was playing poker with a U.S. president or golfing with Babe Ruth.

A series of three golf matches between Cobb and Ruth was arranged to raise money for charity in 1941, long after both men had retired from baseball. After they split the first two matches, Cobb deliberately looked terrible in a practice round and said he had no chance to beat Ruth. The Babe was lulled into overconfidence, and Cobb beat him easily. "I went into those Ruth matches as determined to win as I ever was on the ball field," Cobb said.

Did he ever change? One day, many years after Cobb had notched his last hit and had scored his last run, he was talking with former catcher Nig Clarke in a hotel lobby.

"I had pretty fast hands, Ty," Clarke said. "I brought them down mighty fast in plays at home plate. In fact, many a time the umpire called a runner out even though I never tagged him."

Cobb just smiled.

"Why," Clarke laughed, "there must have been a dozen times when I missed you, Ty, but you were called out."

Suddenly, the enraged Cobb leaped at Clarke and clamped his hands around the man's throat. "Twelve runs you cost me that I earned!" Cobb roared. Three men were needed to pull him off the 53-year-old Clarke. It did not matter to Cobb that he had scored 2,245 runs, more than anyone else ever had. Clarke had gotten the edge on him 12 times, and he could not stand that.

In 1936, Cobb was among the first group of players to be inducted into the Baseball Hall of Fame. Of the many honors he had received, none made him prouder, especially when it was announced that he had gotten more votes than any of the four other players who were inducted: Babe Ruth, Honus Wagner, Walter Johnson, and Christy Mathewson.

In 1942, the *Sporting News* asked the real experts—major league managers and some of the game's greatest players—who was the best player of all time. Cobb received 60 of the 102 votes. The runner-up, Honus Wagner, got only 17.

After retiring from baseball in 1928, Cobb did a lot of hunting and fishing. He went to some ballgames and recommended some players he liked, but he was restless and discontented. He sometimes regretted that he had not become a

*Cobb talks about old times with two of his former Detroit Tigers teammates, Davey Jones (left) and Sam Crawford (center), at a Baseball Hall of Fame banquet in 1957. Cobb was one of the first players to be inducted into the Hall of Fame.*

surgeon and done things to help people. He built a hospital in Royston in honor of his parents and established a scholarship fund for students to go to college. He was able to do these things because he had all the money he needed.

According to his youngest son, James, Ty Cobb was thoughtful and considerate. James was an army sergeant during World War II, and when his ship returned from overseas, landing in San Francisco's harbor, his father was waiting on the dock with a quart of milk and some doughnuts.

"Here," Cobb said, "I know you'll enjoy this."

"He knew how much I liked cold milk," James said later. "It was a simple gesture of thoughtfulness, but it's something I'll never forget."

Cobb could also be a loner, however, and this side of his character eventually cost him the closeness of his own family. In 1947, his wife, Charlie, divorced him. "Maybe," Cobb told a friend, "I was too aggressive and went too far. I always had to be right in any argument, and wanted to be first in everything. . . . If I had done things differently, I would have had more friends."

Cobb married Frances Fairburn Cass two years later. But his second wife, unable to take Cobb's mood swings and temper, divorced him, too. In the years that followed, he spent some time with his grandchildren in Florida and moved about from Georgia to California to Lake Tahoe, Nevada.

In the fall of 1959, Cobb learned he had cancer. He fought that, too, through long bouts in hospitals. He spent the last two years of his life in almost constant pain, but he continued to battle—with the state over taxes and with the electric company over bills.

The fight finally went out of Cobb on July 17, 1961, in Atlanta. He was 74 years old. His first wife and three surviving children were by his side at the time of his death. Three former ballplayers—Mickey Cochrane, Ray Schalk, and Cobb's minor league teammate Nap Rucker— were among the 400 people who attended his funeral in Royston.

When the green Georgia Peach had first arrived in Detroit, his father had written him a letter that ended with these words: "Starve and drive out the evil demon that lurks in all human blood ready to arise and reign. Be under the perpetual guidance of the better angel of your nature."

In his last years, Cobb believed that he had lived up to his father's advice. He remained bitter about all the stories that portrayed him as a dirty, mean, and vicious player who delighted in hurting people. And yet baseball's record book says otherwise: that the better angel of Ty Cobb's nature lost some battles to the demons that drove him relentlessly to be the best.

# CHRONOLOGY

| | |
|---|---|
| 1886 | Born Tyrus Raymond Cobb in the Narrows, Georgia, on December 18 |
| 1904 | Plays for Anniston of the Tennessee-Alabama League and the Augusta Tourists of the South Atlantic League |
| 1905 | Cobb's mother kills his father; the Tourists sell Cobb to the Detroit Tigers for $750; Cobb gets a hit in his first major league at-bat |
| 1906 | Begins a 23-year streak in which he bats .320 or higher each year |
| 1907 | Wins the first of 12 American League batting titles, the first of 8 slugging titles, and the first of 6 stolen-base titles; the Detroit Tigers win the first of 3 consecutive pennants |
| 1908 | Cobb marries Charlie Lombard |
| 1909 | Wins the American League's Triple Crown |
| 1911 | Posts career highs in batting average (.420), base hits (248), runs scored (147), runs batted in (144), and slugging percentage (.621); named the American League's most valuable player |
| 1912 | Suspended for 10 days and fined $50 for beating up a fan |
| 1914 | Becomes baseball's highest-paid player, receiving $15,000 a year |
| 1915 | Sets a major league single-season record by stealing 96 bases |
| 1918 | Enlists in the U.S. Army and becomes a captain in the Chemical Warfare Service |
| 1920 | Named manager of the Detroit Tigers |
| 1925 | Sets an American League single-game record with 16 total bases, on May 5 |
| 1926 | Resigns as manager of the Detroit Tigers after being accused of having fixed a game in 1919 |
| 1927 | Signs with the Philadelphia Athletics; becomes the first player to collect 4,000 career base hits |
| 1928 | Posts a .323 batting average in his last major league season; retires as the all-time leader in games played (3,032), at-bats (11,429), base hits (4,191), runs scored (2,244), stolen bases (892), and batting average (.367) |
| 1936 | Among the first group of players to be inducted into the Baseball Hall of Fame |
| 1947 | Divorces his wife, Charlie |
| 1949 | Marries Frances Fairburn Cass |
| 1961 | Dies of cancer in Atlanta, Georgia, on July 17 |

TYRUS RAYMOND COBB

DETROIT-PHILADELPHIA, A.L.-1905-1928
LED AMERICAN LEAGUE IN BATTING
TWELVE TIMES AND CREATED OR
EQUALLED MORE MAJOR LEAGUE
RECORDS THAN ANY OTHER PLAYER.
RETIRED WITH 4191 MAJOR LEAGUE HITS.

# MAJOR LEAGUE STATISTICS

## DETROIT TIGERS, PHILADELPHIA ATHLETICS

| YEAR | TEAM | G | AB | R | H | 2B | 3B | HR | RBI | BA | SB |
|------|------|-----|-------|------|------|-----|-----|-----|------|------|-----|
| 1905 | DET A | 41 | 150 | 19 | 36 | 6 | 0 | 1 | 15 | .240 | 2 |
| 1906 | | 97 | 350 | 44 | 112 | 13 | 7 | 1 | 41 | .320 | 23 |
| 1907 | | 150 | 605 | 97 | 212 | 29 | 15 | 5 | 116 | .350 | 49 |
| 1908 | | 150 | 581 | 88 | 188 | 36 | 20 | 4 | 101 | .324 | 39 |
| 1909 | | 156 | 573 | 116 | 216 | 33 | 10 | 9 | 115 | .377 | 76 |
| 1910 | | 140 | 509 | 106 | 196 | 36 | 13 | 8 | 88 | .385 | 65 |
| 1911 | | 146 | 591 | 147 | 248 | 47 | 24 | 8 | 144 | .420 | 83 |
| 1912 | | 140 | 553 | 119 | 227 | 30 | 23 | 7 | 90 | .410 | 61 |
| 1913 | | 122 | 428 | 70 | 167 | 18 | 16 | 4 | 67 | .390 | 52 |
| 1914 | | 97 | 345 | 69 | 127 | 22 | 11 | 2 | 57 | .368 | 35 |
| 1915 | | 156 | 563 | 144 | 208 | 31 | 13 | 3 | 99 | .369 | 96 |
| 1916 | | 145 | 542 | 113 | 201 | 31 | 10 | 5 | 68 | .371 | 68 |
| 1917 | | 152 | 588 | 107 | 225 | 44 | 23 | 7 | 102 | .383 | 55 |
| 1918 | | 111 | 421 | 83 | 161 | 19 | 14 | 3 | 64 | .382 | 34 |
| 1919 | | 124 | 497 | 92 | 191 | 36 | 13 | 1 | 70 | .384 | 28 |
| 1920 | | 112 | 428 | 86 | 143 | 28 | 8 | 2 | 63 | .334 | 14 |
| 1921 | | 128 | 507 | 124 | 197 | 37 | 16 | 12 | 101 | .389 | 22 |
| 1922 | | 137 | 526 | 99 | 211 | 42 | 16 | 4 | 99 | .401 | 9 |
| 1923 | | 145 | 556 | 103 | 189 | 40 | 7 | 6 | 88 | .340 | 9 |
| 1924 | | 155 | 625 | 115 | 211 | 38 | 10 | 4 | 74 | .338 | 23 |
| 1925 | | 121 | 415 | 97 | 157 | 31 | 12 | 12 | 102 | .378 | 13 |
| 1926 | | 79 | 233 | 48 | 79 | 18 | 5 | 4 | 62 | .339 | 9 |
| 1927 | PHI A | 133 | 490 | 104 | 175 | 32 | 7 | 5 | 93 | .357 | 22 |
| 1928 | | 95 | 353 | 54 | 114 | 27 | 4 | 1 | 40 | .323 | 5 |
| **Totals** | | 3032 | 11429 | 2244 | 4191 | 724 | 297 | 118 | 1959 | .367 | 892 |

# FURTHER READING

Acocella, Bart, et al. *The All-Time All-Star Baseball Book.* New York: Avon, 1985.

Alexander, Charles C. *Ty Cobb.* New York: Oxford University Press, 1984.

Appel, Marty. *Yesterday's Heroes: Revisiting the Old-Time Baseball Stars.* New York: Morrow, 1988.

Cobb, Ty, with Al Stump. *My Life in Baseball: The True Record.* Garden City, NY: Doubleday, 1961.

Honig, Donald, and Lawrence Ritter. *Baseball: When the Grass Was Real.* New York: Coward, McCann and Geohegan, 1975.

McCallum, John D. *Ty Cobb.* New York: Praeger, 1975.

Macht, Norman L. *Babe Ruth.* New York: Chelsea House, 1991.

———. *Christy Mathewson.* New York: Chelsea House, 1991.

Ritter, Lawrence S. *The Glory of Their Times.* New York: Macmillan, 1966.

———. *The Story of Baseball.* New York: Morrow, 1983.

Seymour, Harold. *Baseball: The Early Years.* New York: Oxford University Press, 1960.

# INDEX

Anniston, Alabama, 23
*Atlanta Journal*, 23
Augusta, Georgia, 21, 22
Augusta Tourists, 21–22, 24
Baker, Frank 37–38
Bennett Park, 29
Bush, Donie, 38
Chalmers Automobile Company, 44–45
Chapman, Ray, 47
Chase, Hal, 10
Chesbro, Jack, 29
Chevrolet, Louis, 42
Chicago Cubs, 38
Chicago White Sox, 9
Civil War, 15
Clarke, Nig, 55
Cleveland Indians, 9
Cobb, Amanda Chitwood (mother), 16, 26–27
Cobb, Beverly (daughter), 41
Cobb, Charlie Lombard (first wife), 41, 56
Cobb, Florence (sister), 16
Cobb, Frances Fairburn Cass (second wife), 57
Cobb, Herschel (son), 41
Cobb, Howell, 15
Cobb, James (son), 41, 56
Cobb, Paul (brother), 16
Cobb, Shirley (daughter), 41
Cobb, Tyrus, Jr. (son), 41
Cobb, Tyrus Raymond
　acting career, 43–44
　birth, 15
　childhood, 16–19
　contracts cancer, 57
　death, 57
　and fans, 38, 45, 47

hobbies, 42
inducted into Hall of Fame, 55
investments, 42–43
manages Detroit Tigers, 49–50
marriages, 41, 57
personality, 26, 32–33, 47
playing style, 30–31, 35–37
plays in minor leagues, 21–25
resigns from Detroit Tigers, 52–53
retires from baseball, 55–56
rookie year in major leagues, 28–31
signs with Philadelphia Athletics, 53
sold to Detroit Tigers, 27
and teammates, 31–32, 45, 46
World War I service, 46
Cobb, William H. (father), 15–16, 18, 21–24, 26–27, 57
Coca-Cola Company, 43
Cochrane, Mickey, 57
*College Widow, The*, 43
Crawford, Sam, 38
Detroit Tigers, 9, 12, 25, 29–33, 35, 37, 38, 45, 46, 47, 49
Edison, Thomas A., 53
Elberfeld, Kid, 30
Elberton, Georgia, 17
Ford, Henry, 42
Gehrig, Lou, 50
General Motors, 43
Hardy, Oliver, 26
Heilmann, Harry, 49
Jackson, Shoeless Joe, 39
Jennings, Hugh, 35, 36, 45, 49
Johnson, Walter, 55
Krichell, Paul, 36
Lajoie, Nap, 44
Landis, Kenesaw Mountain, 52

Laurel, Stan, 26
Lazzeri, Tony, 54
Leidy, George, 25
Leonard, Dutch, 52
Mack, Connie, 53, 54
Mathewson, Christy, 46, 55
Mays, Carl, 47
Moriarty, George, 11
Mullin, George, 38
Narrows, the, Georgia, 15
New York Highlanders. *See* New York Yankees
New York Yankees, 9, 47, 53, 54
Oldfield, Barney, 42
Olds, Ransom, 42
Philadelphia Athletics, 9, 11, 37, 45, 53, 54
Pittsburgh Pirates, 38
Rice, Grantland, 23–24, 44
Rickey, Branch, 37
Royston, Georgia, 16
Royston Reds, 16–17
Royston Rompers, 16
Rucker, Nap, 26, 57
Ruth, Babe, 50–51, 54, 55
Schaefer, Germany, 33
Schalk, Ray, 57
Scott, Everett, 37
*Somewhere in Georgia*, 44
South Atlantic ("Sally") League, 21
Speaker, Tris, 52
Waddell, Rube, 11–13
Wagner, Honus, 55
White, Doc, 30–31
Willett, Ed, 38
World War I, 46

## PICTURE CREDITS

Courtesy Richard Bak:  pp. 14, 17, 20, 24, 25; National Baseball Library, Cooperstown, NY:  pp. 2, 8, 11, 12, 28, 30, 34, 36, 38, 44, 46, 56, 58, 60; *The Sporting News*: p. 32; UPI/Bettmann: pp. 40, 43, 48, 50, 52, 54

NORMAN MACHT was a minor league general manager with the Milwaukee Braves and Baltimore Orioles organizations and has been a stockbroker and college professor. His work has appeared in *The BallPlayers*, *The Sporting News*, *Baseball Digest*, *USA Today*, *Baseball Weekly*, and *Sports Heritage*, and he is the co-author with Dick Bartell of *Rowdy Richard*. Norman Macht lives in Newark, Delaware.

JIM MURRAY, veteran sports columnist of the *Los Angeles Times*, is one of America's most acclaimed writers. He has been named "America's Best Sportswriter" by the National Association of Sportscasters and Sportswriters 14 times, was awarded the Red Smith Award, and was twice winner of the National Headliner Award. In addition, he was awarded the J. G. Taylor Spink Award in 1987 for "meritorious contributions to baseball writing." With this award came his 1988 induction into the National Baseball Hall of Fame in Cooperstown, New York. In 1990, Jim Murray was awarded the Pulitzer Prize for Commentary.

EARL WEAVER is the winningest manager in Baltimore Orioles history by a wide margin. He compiled 1,480 victories in his 17 years at the helm. After managing eight different minor league teams, he was given the chance to lead the Orioles in 1968. Under his leadership the Orioles finished lower than second place in the American League East only four times in 17 years. One of only 12 managers in big league history to have managed in four or more World Series, Earl was named Manager of the Year in 1979. The popular Weaver had his number 5 retired in 1982, joining Brooks Robinson, Frank Robinson, and Jim Palmer, whose numbers were retired previously. Earl Weaver continues his association with the professional baseball scene by writing, broadcasting, and coaching.